The Poetry Project

A collection of poems by kiwi authors

I0176579

Collated by Clare Erasmus and Stacey Broadbent

Published by Koru Press, New Zealand

ISBN: 978-1-0670533-0-7

The Poetry Project

A collection of poems by kiwi authors

Collated by Clare Erasmus and Stacey Broadbent

Contents

Introduction
Author biographies

Introduction

It's with great excitement and pride that we present this beautiful anthology, a true labour of love and collaboration between two passionate Kiwi authors, Clare Erasmus and Stacey Broadbent. Our journey began a few years ago at a Kiwi Author Event that Stacey initiated, and from that moment, we knew we shared not only a deep love for words but also a shared vision of bringing New Zealand's literary voices together.

In the wake of the challenges posed by the COVID-19 pandemic, we were inspired to unite fellow Kiwi authors in a celebration of creativity and resilience. This poetry anthology is the result of that vision—a collection of evocative poems that reflect the rich tapestry of life in Aotearoa. Each piece within these pages represents not only the individual experiences of the authors but also the sense of community that has grown among us as we share our stories, ideas, and reflections through poetic verse.

This anthology is a testament to the power of poetry to connect, to heal, and to inspire. It is more than just a collection of words—it's a network of voices that have come together to celebrate the beauty of our land, our people, and the wide array of human experiences we all share.

As you turn these pages, we hope you are moved by the beauty of our shared creativity and the stories woven together in verse. This collection is a celebration of New Zealand's literary community, and we are incredibly proud to present it to you.

With gratitude and excitement,
Clare Erasmus & Stacey Broadbent

Ehara taku toa i te toa takitahi, engari he toa takitini.
(My strength is not that of an individual, but that of many.)

All proceeds of this anthology will be donated to Ronald McDonald House

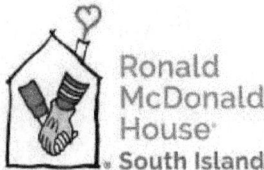

Author Biographies

Will Alexander

Will Alexander is an actor who specialises in Shakespeare. He also teaches children to perform and is currently directing his second film in which all the parts are played by primary school children.

Stacey Broadbent

Stacey Broadbent is a multi-genre author who writes under three names. An avid reader and lover of all things bookish, Stacey has made it her goal to share about her favourite authors and books she's read, while also building her own publishing story. She is a qualified proofreader and is embarking on a new journey of study – Diploma in Library and Information Skills and a Bachelor of Arts.

www.staceybroadbent.com/

Leslie D. Bush

I live in Christchurch, New Zealand. My love of language is eternal. My love of reading goes back to my childhood, writing poems to my youth. Life is poetry; poetry is life. I am a Poet, not just any poet; by nurture and nature; by the fickle finger of fate; by the perversities of chaos, chance and choice; I am unique. Over the last 15 years, I have written over 600 poems, some internationally published.

www.lesliedbushpoetry.nz

Deborah Carter

United Kingdom born, but I've lived in New Zealand for most of my life. I am married with three children and two stepchildren, and so far, a total of twelve beautiful grandchildren.

I work full time for a local firm as receptionist and dispatch manager.

In my limited free time, I love to read. My favourite genres being vampire, shifter, and dark.

http://www.deborahcarterauthor.com/

Marion Day

Marion, an award-winning New Zealand author, crafts stories with a unique Kiwi flair. She resides in the beautiful Marlborough Sounds and writes for adults, with a focus on children and young adults. Marion has thirteen published books and loves to write poetry when inspired.

www.marionday.nz

Clare Erasmus

Clare Erasmus is a versatile author with a passion for multiple genres. Writing poetically since childhood, she has a deep appreciation for figurative language and creative expression. As an educator, author, and researcher, Clare has shared her insights through published books, research articles, poetry, and magazine features for over two decades. Her work reflects a lifelong dedication to storytelling and exploration across various forms of writing.

Joshua Freeman

My job involves diagnosing and treating illness, so I analyse a lot of information and use science to solve practical problems. When work ends I find balance through poetry and music. Poetry and music don't offer practical solutions, but they certainly help me live more expressively and to treasure simple pleasures. I haven't written many poems. Thank you for reading this one.

Sue Glamuzina

Susan Glamuzina is a New Zealand artist who feels at home when there's sand between her toes and her thoughts are in the clouds. Susan's been widely published and won a handful of writing and poetry competitions.

https://linktr.ee/susieleenz

S. N. Goldensnoot

Smudge Noodle Goldensnoot is a Canterbury born greyhound, who competed on track under the name "MELLA YELLA." Deemed too slow to race, Smudge was adopted by an English major and subsequently developed a passion for poetry. His eclectic style is zany, scathing, and heartfelt in turns and has earned him praise as Aotearoa's most promising canine writer. Smudge now resides in Auckland, living - and writing - as a free dog.

instagram.com/s.n.goldensnoot

Warren Grieve

Warren has been a youth group leader, children's ministry leader, drama troupe instigator, and is currently based at Harmony Church in Christchurch, New Zealand.

A digital technologies teacher/specialist by day, he dons extra energy and writes stuff – when not fiddling with digital technologies, he is playing football, reffing touch, or having fun with his grandsons. He has been writing and performing poetry/spoken words since his teenage years.

Susan Howard

Susan Howard is a poet and playwright, living in Matakana. Her poetry reflects her observations of her daily life and the world about her. She has been published in New Zealand and overseas.

Andrene Low

Raised on the whimsical verses of Ogden Nash, Andrene discovered early that words could both delight and subvert expectations. Her love affair with language evolved from childhood scribbles to crafting jokes that made strangers laugh during her time as a stand-up comic. Now a full-time author, she divides her time between writing romance, thrillers, and paranormal mysteries, crafting stories that keep readers turning pages.

https://papersparrowsnest.com/

Hope Mendelssohn

Hope is a singer, composer, conductor and writer based in the Waikato. Her music [both sacred and secular] has been published, performed, recorded and broadcast internationally. She has written poetry for adults, young adults and children for whom she has also written a series of short stories. The children's literature is suitable for ages 7 years upwards. Hope has studied the arts at both the University of Auckland and the University of Waikato.

Chanelle Muirhead

Chanelle Muirhead is a stage manager who has worked with The Pop-Up Globe, NZ Opera and the Sydney Arts Festival. She enjoys surfing, singing and playing the piano. Chanelle writes a lot of poetry however this is the first time her poetry has been published.

Deryn Pittar

Deryn Pittar is an award-winning author. She writes across a wide range of genres; sci-fi/fantasy, contemporary, young adult, and a dash of horror. She loves the challenge of short and flash fiction, and dabbles in poetry. Her newsletter will drop a piece of short fiction into your inbox about once a month.

Free reads newsletter: https://iwriteuread.substack.com

https://www.amazon.com/author/derynpittar

Sally Pugh

Sally Pugh lives in Whanganui with her partner and three dogs. She spends her time dreaming, teaching, painting, reading, and sometimes writing. She is an armchair traveller and is passionate about wildlife and protecting the natural environment. Her Instagram is

Sally.af.pugh@instagram

Johanna M. Rae

Author Johanna Rae is a former fashion designer, wife, and mother. She lives with her family, and two adorable ragdoll cats named Macchiato and Smudge. Balancing family life and her writing schedule doesn't always leave much time for leisure, but in the quiet moments, Johanna can be found with her nose in a book or crocheting up a storm.

https://www.johannamraeauthor.com/

Michelle Rooke

Michelle is a writer hailing from Nelson, New Zealand (Whakatū, Aotearoa), currently based in Melbourne (Naarm). She acquired an interest in writing from a young age and finds solace and sanctity in expressing herself in a variety of verbal mediums.

Tessa Sillifant

A lover of life with a thirst for knowledge and adventure, Tessa is the author of The Twists and Turns of a Traveller: Life Lessons, Adventures, and Everything in Between. Tessa has also had work published in the Auckland Writers Tales of the Domain short fiction and poetry book and is the creator of COLINCU – a wellbeing themed e-zine that aims to support, inspire, and empower.

Peter Speakman

Peter Speakman is an Auckland-born specialist in tax and company law. Passionate about the outdoors, he particularly enjoys mountain activities. He is also a proud father of three young men, who are described as wonderfully unassuming. His blend of professional expertise and love for nature shapes his grounded, dynamic approach to life.

Katrina Ward

Katrina Ward is an educator, artist and writer living and working in Taranaki, New Zealand who always has something creative on the boil. She has taught Visual Arts, Art History and English in secondary schools and also freelances as an education consultant. Her passions include poetry, painting, plants and pedagogy and she believes that life is lived best in full colour.

www.katrinawardcreative.com

Raewyn Whyte

Raewyn Whyte lives on the edge of Hokianga Harbour, surrounded by ever-changing vistas of land, sea, sky. After many years of writing about dance performance, her focus has shifted to the performances outside her windows.

Angela Woolf

Angela enjoys writing contemporary and speculative fiction novels, short stories, and poems, and her work has received several placings in competitions in New Zealand.

Her most recent work is the anthology Rere Takitahi Flying Solo she co-edited with good friend Jenny Purchase, released in July 2024.

The inspiration for the poem 'Grace' was Patricia Grace DCNZM QSO who was a speaker at the Marlborough book festival is 2022. On the drive home, she understood that poetry might be the best form of recording a difficult story she'd tried many times to write.

Find Angela on FB as AJ Woolf
https://www.facebook.com/ajwoolf007

Whispers

Clare Erasmus

Your whispers,
A fresh breath of crisp air,
Enlighten my heart.
Like a clock wound up,
I swirl and prance
And for a moment…
Glimmers of hope.

Trickles of hope,
Sprinkled within,
Nourish my soul.
Lighting my fire,
Full of desire
Your whispers.

The Writer

Stacey Broadbent

Weaving magic with only words,
A writer's voice can be heard,
Turning phrases to describe,
All the world seen from their eyes.

Painting pictures you can see,
Drawing from a memory.
Images of childhood fun,
Of finding faith; seeing the sun.

What you see inside your head,
Is but an image they have led,
With perfectly descriptive prose,
So you can see what they propose.

And that, dear reader, you will find,
Is what pushes the writer's mind.
For an author's voice needs only this;
To send their reader into bliss.

Grace

Angela Woolf

I've become a poet
so I can blurt out the lines that come in anger
and not sweat the details
that aren't important
Quick and short and easy to undo
like a crochet blanket
A poem every sunset, every moon rise
as a measure of time
to tell the story I've tried ten times
to write
but failed
It takes short burst of rage to make sense
when there is none
And there is no forgiveness
because it's too late
after the darkness
takes a soul

Reflection

Tessa Sillifant

Reflecting on what I couldn't see, the first-time round
I look at the love I lost and the love I found
Feeling the tears trickle away to an unreachable zone
As I let go of the past, and all that was known
Stepping backwards to keep moving forward
I am blessed with life's rewards
This is who I am today
See me, believe me; let me have my say
Reflecting on who I am and being proud
I look at the love I lost and the love I have found
I am stronger and wiser; I am kind
I let myself feel love inside my mind
Striving forward with glances back
I am blessed with life's rewards
This is who I am today
See me, hear me; I am not going away
Reflecting on the world and those that are around
I look at the love I lost and the love I have found
Surrounded by clarity, hope and peace
I let the dark clouds around me cease
Leaping forward with a quick glance back
I am blessed with life's rewards
This is who I am today
I am seen, I am heard; living life, my way!

Silence

Hope Mendelssohn

Silence breaks upon me
And tomorrow washes away
For today is the answer that we're looking for
Look around you, what could be more
Beautiful than this, tell me what you'd miss
If you left your favourite shore?
Golden sands, love-locked hands
And watered feet
Wind-blown souls, chartered hearts
Prepare our wake
When the gull cries see Him watching over you
When the shell breaks hear me cry
I hear your voice on the crest of our wave
I feel your arms reaching out to me
So tell me you want nothing more than this
Look around you, isn't this bliss
Silence that surrounds us
Beauty in our wake.

Irresistible

Johanna M Rae

Deliciously decadent
Beckoning like a forbidden culinary masterpiece
Tempting like none other preceding it
Smooth and luxurious
Silky, yet sweet
Sinful, but satisfying
Irresistible and ripe for the picking
Yearning to be mine

Shuffling closer
Common sense is all but abandoned
Woefully unnecessary
An exorbitant price
Longing betrays me
Willpower dissipates
I am losing the battle
I must have it

Perfectly perfect
It greets me with glorious purpose
As if it was made only for me
Heaven against my skin
Opulent, yet simple
Meticulous but uncomplicated
The scales have tipped
I bought the gosh-darned dress

When I'm 86...

Andrene Low

I will own 37 cats. All black and white. All called Tiddles.
Confusing the neighbours with their muttered counting.
I will boldly state, "I only have the one, but he's very fast."

My house will be decorated in wall-to-wall grey.
Some of the carpet Axminster: most of it Tiddles.
I'll be able to lose myself in the soft furnishings.

When I die, the Tiddles will live off me two full months.
The funeral money appropriated.
For counselling.
For cleaning.
For cat food.

How Santa nearly broke our family

Deborah Carter

Santa's feet are in the hearth, with his sugar plums in sight
Our Rottweiler, Dex, licks his chops, just hankering for a bite
I left a note of warning, upon the chimney pot
I guess Santa never read it, and now he's in a spot.
He deserves a little discomfort; I feel it's kind of fair
After the mess he left here last year, size 12 footprints on the stair
Mum thought that I'd been messy, and punished me for the crime
It didn't matter that I pointed out; my shoe is just size nine.
Now Santa's knees are shaking, his fear is palpable
Wondering if I'll help him, or let my dog chomp on his ball
I note I'm on the nice list and make my mind up in a hurry
Pushing past my puppy, and to Santa I do scurry
"Come on Santa, bend your knees, I'll help you from the hearth
The tree's just there, the lights all lit, see, I've cleared a path"

One, two three, four gifts, "Is that all I get?" I hissed
"I just saved your bollocks!" I was well and truly pissed.
He turned around and eyed my dog and then gave me a
glare
Held his empty sack up, to show nothing else was there
Disappointment filled my body, and my stomach hit the
floor
And Santa took advantage and scuttled toward the door
"Um, I don't think so Santa, that's not how you came
in"
Dex sidled past to guard the door, makes me want to
grin
"Up the chimney, Santa. With tradition we must uphold
So, step on up and touch your nose, if you'd be so bold"
With a shake of his head, he walks to me and tugs his
beard down
"It's me, your dad, not Santa Clause," my brows turn to
a frown
He whispers, "Santa isn't real, luv. I dress up, it's all a
ruse
"So, they were your size 12 last year, I got blamed for"
I accuse.
His mouth turned down and his head drooped low as he
shook it back and forth
"You've seen my shoes; they are size 10," now that gave
me a pause
If it wasn't him and it wasn't me, then who came to our
house that day
A jangling sound came from the roof, "Could that be
Santa's sleigh?"

Dad grabbed me quick, and sofa dived, and covered us with a rug

Santa slithered down to the hearth, and gave his sack a tug

It landed with a heavy thump as it hit the wooden floor

And we watched as Santa darted round, and checked behind the door

Satisfied he'd not been heard, he tipped his heavy sack

One by one, gaily wrapped, each present neatly stacked

Job well done, he ate the cookie and took a swig of drink

His roving eye ran round the room, and I swear he gave a wink

Had we been found I wondered, as Dad held me quietly in place

To be caught spying on Santa Clause would be a big disgrace

'Oh, oh, oh' he grumbled, as he turned without a care

And for a man so heavy, he fair pelted up those stairs

We didn't move a muscle; we just waited, one minute, two

And Santa could be heard above, as he finished and flushed the loo

Then back he came to collect his sack and into the hearth he bent

With a loud 'Ho Ho Ho' he touched his nose and up the chimney he went

Dad stood slowly, his mouth agape and turned an eye to me

But I was busy looking at the mass of gifts beneath our tree

"He's real," I said "Can you believe it?" I turned toward my dad

And for the very first time in this whole year, his face, it wasn't sad

He entered the hall and stared at the steps, a size 12 footprint or two are there

Like the one that had been there a year ago, the same print upon the stair

So much fighting and accusations, it was still an open case

Now his eyes are bright with unshed tears, but a smile lights up his face

"Get to bed and take Dex too, it's time that you were sleeping"

He followed me up, and then peeled off, to the room where mum was weeping

He told her the story, of what had him worried, shared with her his fear

He pulled her in and hugged her tight, and wiped away a tear

Christmas morning came and went, unwrapped gifts, and bellies well fed

Darkness came, we climbed the stairs, husband and wife slipped into bed

As they made love she chuckled with mirth, at the story she did recall

How her husband as Santa got stuck in the hearth, and Dex nearly chewed off his balls.

Contemplating the Quiet Life

Susan Howard

The flower garden
by the house
has to fend for itself
these days.
A wilderness of
bird scattered
self-seeds,
and inconsiderate
rambling roses.

The herb garden however,
has become an oasis
amongst the wildflowers.

Here I plant for meals
not yet planned.
Parcel because it tastes like
celery in the salad,
rocket or lemon grass,
and now Thai basil
for that new recipe with
lamb meatballs.

Though sometimes
you just have to let life
sail on without you.

Rippling

Raewyn Whyte (Opara, August 2022)

The harbour is glassily calm today
No wind, not even a gentle breeze
Wispy clouds above
bright sunshine
So still you can see the fish jumping
Breaking the surface so briefly
To feed or perhaps just for pleasure
Glinting in the sun
Leaving ripples as they submerge again

The Delusion of Inaction

Peter Speakman

A cold wind weathered her face
Adding to her pervading sense of doom
Turmoil burgeoning,
her resilience feverishly trying but unable to keep apace
Ahead, her eyes were affixed with gloom
Apprehension rang loud
A change of direction strongly in need
 She resiled to her visage that was proud
To the warnings, she paid no heed
Obstinacy and fear of the unknown
Gripping her, shunting her away from the path shown
Belief that comfort lay in hanging onto the past
Doubtful that her spirit to change would last
Convinced that solace would be hers by decree
Resoundingly confining her to what is and what should
never be.

Home

Chanelle Muirhead

Just like the moon
pulls back the hungry tide
licking the shore,

why does it seem impossible
that you call to me the same way?

Slowly drawing back my layers
until the parts of me
that once were part of you
see each other,

sigh, and say:

"Ah, home."

Grief

Warren Grieve

Why
do we run from
the pain
the betrayal
the deep loss,
disappointment,
Run to Hide
to shield minds from hurt
Escape to deal with it on
our own,
and in the silent screams
blame the good
blame the truth
Adopt broken friends
with drug answers
with party distractions
with distorted ideas,
bury self in business
discover an addiction,
Yet somehow
the pain doubles
scraping our skull
scaring our soul darker
allowing disillusionment
to embed.

We can start
from the stolen now,
be real in the pain
scream out the overwhelming
Look to the mountains
Look in the eyes
of a child
see and smell depths
of wonder in a flower
Hear something different,
Embrace the despair
Face the pain
and look to God
to grace the pain,
And in a step
a brief clarity
a fingernail opening
space in the grim,
cry for something new
within the uncontrolled,
we can find
a comforter
a God who knows

depths of pain
Who has crossed
from Heaven to
human heartache
The love of a God
Who gave us

the pain of Jesus
Resurrection power in Jesus.
Allow God
to show you
His surrounding arms of joy
to embed your life
with love
To encircle you with
Eternal Hope…
And life will grow
around
and through Grief.

Resonate

Clare Erasmus

Your voice of wisdom,
A beacon of sage advice,
Echoes through the corridors of my mind,
Reminding me to keep my gaze
Fixed on the goal.

And though the goal
May shift and reshape,
Your timeless words
Resonate within me.

To know you
Is to have truly lived;
To live is to have been
Guided,
My unwavering compass.

Though my navigation
Has not always been straightforward,
You've guided me—
My map,
My anchor.

I wonder if you
Know,
Just how deeply
You
Resonate.

Questions, and more Questions

Leslie D. Bush

Questions? Questions? Questions?
Does nobody have an answer?
I mean, an answer. Not conjecture
Speculation, hypothesising.

In the data age, we are spoiled
For and with access to information.
How many of us have the skill to process it?
Sort it out, prioritise it according to source

And thus reliability? Not many! Probably even fewer
In times to come! What an <expletive> tragedy.
When the illiterate are forced to face an ocean of
information;
Differing analysis, alternative explanations;
contradictions

How are they to find their way through?
"Ockham's Razor"? "All things being equal (yes?)
We should favour the approach that assumes the least.
(also known as the principle of parsimony.)

Does that help? William of Ockham, an English Friar
Had a predilection towards the metaphysical.
"Assumes the least" might not mean what you thought.
Try this, there are levels of truth, relative to their
experience,

And evidence. There are truths self-defined by descent
and use.
Things are not what they seem. Alice found that out.
What is happening? What is this? Simple questions.
There's a torrent of information waiting to come at
you.

You have to sort out the "truth". Feel confident?
Let's have go. Let's have a try.

I Can't Can

Sally Pugh (not a poet)

Sometimes
You jump in the deep end
Without realising it's the deep end,
And it's too late to say
"I can't".
If you knew what you were getting yourself into
Before you got yourself into it,
There's no way you would have jumped.
You would have walked away,
Saying, "It's too hard. I can't."
But by jumping in
With blissful ignorance
You quickly discover
"I can."

Damsel

Tessa Sillifant

Say the word damsel
and distress echoes in your ears.
An unmarried woman,
who isn't beyond her years.
The view of being saved,
is conjured within the mind.
Yet she is brave and capable,
more than just kind.
We view others
from our worldview
and our very own eyes.
But what lies beneath
can be
heavily
disguised.
Hard working,
courageous,
day in,
day out.
Is it time to give the damsel,
a celebratory shout?
To our brothers,
daughters,
our families
and our friends.

Is it time to flip the narrative
to a positive lens?
Language is a powerful tool
that can reframe the pictures painted.
So let's work together
to get the damsel reacquainted!

Withheld

S.N. Goldensnoot

Withhold yourself, my son

He said

Put your brain in your chest
And your heart in your head
Leave *before* behind
For now
You've been offered love
But do you know how?
Will you let life teach you
To let love reach you?
Will you open
In hope of closure?
Don 't you know that
You ' re in a trance?
Can you taste the questions
You wish her to answer?
Will you listen a while to me, my son?
And forgive the future
For what the past has done?
Be still, my son

He said to me

Don't take what *could*
For what *must* **be**

Tomorrow is a New Day

Stacey Broadbent

When money is so tight
That you worry how you'll pay,
Just smile and remember,
Tomorrow is a new day.

When you're up at night with fevers
And you want to go to bed,
Just smile and remember,
You have a roof over your head.

When you sleep through your alarm
And you're late for work again,
Just smile and remember,
There's no rainbow without rain.

When there are deadlines at your back
And you feel you're out of time,
Just smile and remember,
You're actually doing fine.

When everything goes wrong
And nothing goes your way,
Just smile and remember,
Tomorrow is a new day.

Seed

Susan Glamuzina

In the dark
alone
buried
underground
I reach out
extend my feet
root support
stretch my arms
reach
grow
finally
I break out
feel the natural heat
secure my feet
as I expand
forming leaves
then a bud
which gets bigger
and bigger
blooms
I follow the sun
till I wilt
then my child
drops
in the dark

alone
buried
underground
he reaches out

Madam Lies ~ Palmist to the Stars

Andrene Low

I gaze at the hand I'm holding
until creases form words,
telling me when,
showing me why.

They never come when they're happy;
only when they're sad,
lost or bewildered.

Wretched and hollow,
her eyes are a rainbow of pain;
the left yellow and purple,
the right black.
She prays for anything
more palatable than reality.

I hedge,
telling of meaningless events,
things she already knows,

bad peppered with good.
Adages rehearsed, repeated
and later regretted.

Watching her despair
rinsed away by cleansing tears,
I take on her emptiness.

This is easier than shattering dreams
and dealing in fear.

She crosses my palm with AMEX
and bounces out of the door,
forcing another shadow
to darken my soul.
Smoothing the velvet cloth
that hides the scarred table beneath,
I listen for the screech of brakes
and a life-ending thud.

Mirror Image?

Deborah Carter

The waves roll in above my head,
Blues blend into grays
Grays shimmer to foamy white
As the wind blows them away.
I stand beneath the trees in autumn,
Staring skyward at bared branches,
As they mirror its hidden roots,
In plain view above my head.
I wonder!

When I'm gone and planted below
With people walking above me,
Will I look up to see the tree's roots
As once mirrored above ground
expecting them to blossom?
Or live my death in Forever Autumn?

Doing Business with Death

Susan Howard
(First published Takahē Magazine 88 December 2016)

I visited the crematorium today, purely on business. We
were scoping a pet cremation service. The manager
watched my face as he went into great detail about the

calcinator chamber in the kiln that continues turning the
body into ashes and how the big bones need to go into a
cremulator after that so it can turn them into dust. First,

place the buckles and other metal objects in that bucket
over there. A baby is watched over carefully as it burns,
because the ashes might get blown all around the kiln,

oh, and how those ashes in the end only cover a space
the size of man's thumb. You just sweep them up
carefully and place them in a thimble. Coming back to

the animals, no pacemakers please they could blow the
kiln sky high as well as kill a man. We discussed if you
throw the bodies in or place them gently, and what to do

with the ashes afterwards. He has a pit for bones and ashes and if that got full he could always dig another one and I tried not to think of Auschwitz.

De-Plen-I-Shed

Clare Erasmus

The World is Angry
It screams and **SHOUTS**
A storm of fury in every sound.

"You've taken too much!"
My oceans drained, my skies turned grey,
My natural resources
Are
De-plen-i-shed.

I shed a tear,
But you don't hear—
The world's voice drowns out your apathy.

"You're hurting me!"
My rivers dry, my air grows thin,
You've stripped my forests bare—
Once a sanctuary
For creatures, critters,
Life now lost in hollowed woods.

The winds howl louder:
You've taken too much!"
My natural wonders,
Are
De-plen-i-shed.

What will you leave behind?
Ashes of greed, or seeds of care?
Before my voice fades
And all that's left is a whisper
In the air.

An Echo

Chanelle Muirhead

In time, your presence will soften.
You will exist only in the echo of laughter,
the crease of a smile.

You will be seen in the tilt of a head
and, more than anything,
in the way they dance.

So, my friend,
though we may not always recognize you,
you will endure.

Desperation

Johanna M Rae

I could run away now
But where would I go
There is nowhere to escape
This life that I know
So misunderstood
So desperate to be free
Pitifully craving
Another like me

An escalation of tension
As my heart threatens to burst
Forever is a long time
To smile away the hurt
The pressure of conformity
Cripples my spine
My spirit is broken
Freedom will never be mine

Immigration

Clare Erasmus

We journeyed.
Cowardly they proclaimed,
And turbulent was the flight.
Cascading down my cheeks
Tears rolled on and on.
And my frown told my journey
Of grieving for family
Left behind,
Into the newness of the world,
The paradise serenely beckoned
Me,
Inviting me.
The newness was raw
Like an existence with no identity.
With no shared history
No root in sight.
But the blossom flourished
Petal, by petal, by petal
Anchored now by
A root created
Just by
Us.

A Question of Colour

Leslie D. Bush

A question of colour; of what: our skin, our sin, our shame;

Things that haunt us and answer to no name. Colour?

I have been watching a television series (in colour? Yes.).

The lead character is a black man. Set me thinking.

I'm not black, brown, yellow or pink. Wait, pink, maybe–

On the pale side, sort of white. OK, I Admit it; I'm white.

Why should that be uncomfortable to admit? I am that I am.

No excuses, justifications or rambling "reasons". Reasons; treasons!

Whatever our immediate situations, parents married,

divorced or decreased, we are born into one family: humanity.

Humanity, with its vanity, profanity, and inanity; humanity displaying

Its sense of vision, hope, faith, indecision; humanity at its worst

And best. Utterly bewildering, frustrating, heartbreaking, and confusing.

Humanity is the collective. We compose the collective.

All of us; regardless

Of nationality, politics, faith, belief system; yes, all of us, regardless of colour;

Be it black, brown, yellow or pink. Yes? No? Maybe? What do you think?

Compartmentalise

Michelle Rooke

I'm sitting in the box you taught me how to make myself
fit inside of
It is sound and small and holds my weight like fragile
eggs in a nest
I hear the cadence of the rain wash away the day's
watercolour pain
I have been painting a mäelstrom of my own malcontent
in an attempt to express
To shed my shadow like a cicada shell in March
I am blue like cold winter light in June
My fingers and feet frozen
The tip of my nose too
I miss the larches golden hue
I envision sentiments of youth and fragmented fragrant
memories
They flood me, like a cumulus shroud of nostalgia
Drawn in silver linings and freeze frames
I've lost pace, weary footwork and loose frays
We are always losing something or we are afraid
I struggle to let go
I feel like a sims character in a swimming pool where
the ladder has been deleted
Treading water
I want to live in verbs but I struggle to find my words
I drown everything in abstraction, too many adjectives

To make sense of anything
I love complexity but I yearn for simplicity
Give me the window pane crisp golden edged light cast just right
Nothing on my mind
Quiet, slow moments that ripple in tune to chords striken with subtle hue, deeply soothe the grooves in my brain like a dark emerald green cape
Somewhere to feel safe, cloaked in comfort a cocoon of one-ness
I pass through the day in witness
Surely there is not enough time to whittle away in listlessness
But I enlist for this in a roundabout fashion through dissociative fracturing
To tap out of a despairing afternoon
Spliffs, snacks and shows
Gorging myself on defeat
Consuming all of my grief
I will put off my guilt till the setting of the moon
And then use it like a spark travelling up a fuse
That the sun has awoken with a boom

I'm sitting in the box you taught me how to make myself fit inside of
I have started to name my emotions as I feel them
I can count all of the ways they are driving me insane
I can feel my body in ways I never realised
There is a pulse in my stomach when I wake up, after I eat, and when I can't sleep

I have lost my stomach falling back into and out of dreams
I used to drive off cliffs in them, now I just get bitten by dogs that don't let go, and bite your hand that feeds me love, or betrayal, or both
I am a witnessing
I am slowly learning how to compartmentalise like you
I am learning not to call or msg or expect you to care
I am forgetting my lessons in the depths of despair
I am scattered pieces on the floor you have forgotten what you are looking for as you walk into the room
But looking at that mess it mustn't be me
You might cut your hands if you tried to reach me
For months I continued to bleed
I am the stain in the carpet that won't come out

Hear Christmas

Warren Grieve

Snow falls
Sounds of silence whisper of
white grace
Cleansing complete,
Stop to the stillness,
listen to the Christ massed voice,
Hushed within
a soft sense of Serene, alone.
undisturbed by thought,
Listen to the Silence in your mind
Hear Christmas.

Sunshine falls
Loves warm Light
Wrapping your heart's pulse.
Holding your hope
Infusing joy undisturbed by thought,
listen to the Silence in your heart,
~the still small voice.
Hear Christmas.

Stars night shine,
Galaxies remote and vast
transfixed reflections in your eyes,
Seeing distance
Feeling closeness of creation
undisturbed by thought,
listen to the silence in your heart,
The rhythm of sustaining life
Hear Christmas

Time to Fly

Hope Mendelssohn

To spread your wings
To view the ocean
From a different perspective

To see the shadows
That lie beneath the cool blue
Of its calm

Yet deceptive surface
To ponder the depths
Of its soul

As you would any other
Who dares to allow you entry
To its world of mystery

And of love
Journeyed by many
Yet treasured by few

Misunderstanding its depths
And sudden changes in direction
Navigating its current

Something beyond logical deduction
Something of which very few
Have access

Too many closed doors
Preventing them from travelling
Down the length of its corridor

Or that which connects us
To another soul
Only fear preventing them

From unlocking that door
In case they will find
The water's touch

Just so sensuous
They can't go back
Through that door

To a life of no nurturing,
No mystery, no soul
And no love.

Slow Rain

Raewyn Whyte (Opara, July 2022)

The rain advances slowly
across the harbour
transitioning from threat to lashing
against the windows
The clouds layer up
progressively
obscuring the landscape
champing on the tops of the coastal range
slowly filling the valleys
til four stacked ridges
vanish

The Unmoored

Chanelle Muirhead

Somewhere out there,
the sun shines on you—
eyes creasing, hair swept back.

And in that parallel universe,
I recognize you
by the warmth of your heart
before I even know your name.

It is a different time,
a different place,
where fear does not stop your hand
from reaching for mine,
and hesitation does not
hold. my. tongue.

There,
the sound of your easy laughter
skips across the wind,
and not across my memories.

Out there, somewhere,
is a kinder life
where I am not unmoored—
because you are still in it.

As I Searched, I Found

Clare Erasmus

Oh, what a road I thought I'd travel,
Duly unfair,
To me.
The search for who I was
Pulled me in
To the place I
Should be.

Slowly and surely,
It was I that
I found.
Hello,
Pleased to meet
ME.

This Little Thing

S.N. Goldensnoot

This little thing that lovers bring
                Sometimes stings,
        Sometimes finds wings.

        This little thing can fling you far
Or keep you put
Right where you are.

This lovers' thing - this little piece
                Can stop right now
        Or never cease.

        This *little* lovers' *tiny* thing
Is rather **LARGE**...
I'm beginning to think.

Climate Change

Marion Day

Hurt in the mind
I'd walk to the shore
And sit in the seat my ex (who dumped me)
Had carved from old man pine.

The sea tickled my feet.
Taking the edge off my pain
Now it tickles my bum
Still relieving the ache

I'm determined to persevere
To sit on my loveseat,
To numb the heartache
Until I'm swallowed whole.

A Muriel Spark Life

Susan Howard
(First published Takahē Magazine 95 April 2019)

That might work.
 Her characters move unfettered
 from partner to partner and back again
          without a backward glance or explanation.

As if relationships were like takeaways
 to be picked through,
eaten then discarded,
or a series of rooms
          to be lived in like a hotel or a holiday.

You could live separate lives,
 meet occasionally for good sex.
 Keep the spark alive so to speak
while you seek out
          a lighthouse flashing the sea,

or maybe just a row
 of tea lights dotting the dark
to guide you along the escape route,
          while your partner sets a light in the window.

This is Who I am

Johanna M Rae

Soft, gentle twilight
Darkness brings bliss
Wrapped in anonymity
Come evening's first kiss
Slip away daylight
And let me be free
Dancing in the moonlight
Uninhibited by thee

Beneath the starry cloak of night
Sanctuary is given
Concealed from judgment
Casting fear into oblivion
Standing taller than a mountain
Unfurling my soul to the sky
This is who I am
No more fighting not to cry

Morning Walk

Joshua Freeman

With a faint drone
The timeless spell of cut grass
Ascended from soft, strewn tufts
In the gentlest warmth
It floated through the tree-aura
And predictably settled
It made me think of your inquiring eyes

I've Got This

Clare Erasmus

With a tear on my shoulder
I can do without this.
Watch me as I find my stand
My heart yearns for rest
Yearning for a meaningful touch
My soul desires to dance
Arms freely as I dance in the rain
Swirling to the song
Carelessly
I wait to run into the wild
Like a shooting star
Free me

The cracks were in the wall
The glue was drying out
My eyes were dry
The crying had stopped
I could not
Anymore
The arrowed words spun
Out of control
They scarred me to the soul

And there in front of me, he stood
I recklessly just looked ahead
Gentle nudges
A breath of air
To gently guide me on
The past is gone.
Standing aside its time to take my path
As I move
on

I'm spinning, dizzy
I am dreaming wildly, without breath.
I reach for the door out.
And I'm dancing and laughing
Watch
As I sing
In the light,
Laugh in the rain
And I
Just
Don't
care.

A Question of Taste

Leslie D. Bush

Here comes the doozy
The $6.95 question
Why on earth do you wear such drab clothes?
"Drab clothes?" declare I. What do you mean?

The fight is on. There's conflict in the air!
(I thought that was air freshener, silly me.)
No sir, 'tis the smell of battle, of carnage released
This must be resolved at all costs. We will have no peace

Questions of "taste", why we prefer something
Choose something to wear or exhibit is a no-win situation
The principal pronoun is "I".
"I" want to wear to this. "I" want to show off having this

"You have a problem? Guess what, honey; it's all yours
No one else is interested. BOOM"
Welcome to stage 2 of questions, conflict
Stage 3, a wise choice: conflict resolution

There will be things and styles you detest
You have no choice or decision in them
So you have to bite your lip: mutter a sullen "I
disapprove
But it is your choice. I respect it" and "Must go!"

Is there a question of taste? Maybe there are only
answers

Night Life

Andrene Low

Swaying down the footpath on platforms
that over-shadow their seventies forebears,
your laughter is brittle, your smile tentative.

Legs of a colt, dress of a child, you text those
not present. Posting selfies and stumbling in
your overloaded, pre-loaded state.

$10 in the right cup, dad's credit card in
the left, key hidden in the garden.
You step lightly upon this earth.

Dancing and teasing, you circle a copper.
His hat, yours for glorious seconds. Immortalised
on Facebook. Tagged and shared.

Swirling and twirling, you check out the skinny boys
in their skinny jeans. Slung low. Waist by cheek. Crotch
by knee. Penguins all.

Sway descends to clip-clopping stagger, the
alco-pops want out. "Catch ups" splash back from amid
the discarded coffee cups and old newspapers.

Sleep tugs. Beckoning as sweetly as the bench by the bin. Its smooth length anchors the spinning even when you close your eyes.

But the surface turns against you. Cold and hard. Sterilised stainless. No card, no money, no clothes. You've been tagged again. Jane Doe.

More Than Once

Chanelle Muirhead

I have loved you more than once in this lifetime.

The first time, insistently tugging at my hair
to see if I noticed—
as if my heart could mistake
how easily it fell into your hands.

Once, quietly, floating like the whisper of a memory,
a gentle tune hanging in the air
of a warm summer's night.

Later, effortlessly,
with your arms at home around my waist
and your laughter lingering on my tongue.

Then, confidently, knowing you stitched up parts of me
so often that corners of my heart
have become more you than me.

Now, as inevitable as the changing seasons,
I will love you again—softly, perhaps, for a time.

Two souls intertwined as if they always have been,
no matter the paths taken.

A Fine Drive to Stratford

Katrina Ward

I just follow the mustard lines
And ignore the mountain on my right
Dressed up in teal and cobalt, he tries to steal the show.
Today he competes with the sky.
It is all made up, bruisey purply beautiful
Deep lilac, then ochre
And brightly glazed with dazzling pink.
Even the clouds look like silver-top-milk.
Further on, the mountain
Peeps out from behind sprays of cloud
Expands his turquoise chest
Flashing to Pīhanga beyond.
But I notice that someone has cut their hedge
And that the flaxes look navy today
And that they make a sublime backdrop
For the day-glo dabs of road cones.
Then I see my favourite:
The solitary bull
Just standing, luminous.
Framed in a fresco of green
He is a backlit Bond - stoic, poetic
Facing the day head on.
And I notice the mustard lines again
The destination ahead
Steer another corner
Drive the last stretch
And arrive, full.

Autumn Daze

Stacey Broadbent

Pink cheeks, cold nose,
Breath puffing out like mist.
Hands tucked in pockets,
Fingers in a fist.

Beanie pulled down over ears,
Scarf around the neck.
Thick socks, warm boots;
Everything in check.

Leaves of orange and of red,
Crunching beneath feet.
Trees no longer dressed in green;
Their clothes spread like a sheet.

Hews of gold and amber,
The sky darkens to grey.
Quickened steps, down the path,
On this chilly autumn day.

Up ahead a library glows
With warm lights through the pane,
And scattered all about the place
Are books to feed the brain.

Scarf and hat discarded,
Curled upon a corner chair,
Descending into fantasy;
A land so far from here.

Escape the chill of autumn breeze
Inside a book of spring,
Where flowers bloom, the sky is blue,
And birds begin to sing.

While outside it gets colder,
The sun no longer high,
A world between the pages
Makes the time go by.

And when the journey's over,
The last page turned to close,
Scarf and hat are donned again,
Cool air tickling the nose.

Head tucked against the wind,
Back down the path once more,
Through the gate and up the steps,
Rushing through the door.

Home sweet home, or so they say,
Though I have to disagree.
The library with all its books
Is where I'd rather be.

When Love Runs Out

Clare Erasmus

When you're feeling lost and unsure,
And thoughts swirl around, moving ever so slow,
When your heart still beats, but just barely flows,
That's when you know.

It's hard to let go and embrace the free,
Yet deep down, you sense it's not meant to be.
When a future feels distant, with no light to see,
That's when you know.

When the words that once flowed have all run dry,
And you long for their warmth, but silence replies,
You start to wonder if love can still rise.
That's when you know.

It has been fun, wonderfully wild,
You brought forth my inner, excited child.
So many moments of laughter, so many smiles,
Yet there were times when I just knew.

When I realize it can't go on,
You still fill my heart with a glorious song,
But our feet have stopped dancing, the rhythm is gone—
That's when I just knew.

For me, there are no regrets, I'm sure,
You were my joy, my perfect cure.

Unrequited Love

Deborah Carter

She sings her song so sweetly, A seduction, just for him
She cocks her head and coyly winks, A ploy to sucker
him in
Her beauty is unparalleled, as she dances on her stage
Her head-dress filled with colour, He's enticed toward
her cage
But his love is unrequited, though he tries his very best
He buys her treats and presents, which she accepts, his
love, she tests
But her love is for another, Whom her heart beats
quickly for
Her song gets even louder when her true love knocks the
door
Posing pretty, her chest puffed out, her eyes are all a
sparkle
A little like Prince Harry, when he's eying Megan
Markle
Their kissing sound affects the man, As it's not some
simple peck
He watches with some jealousy, as she nuzzles at her
neck
$400 bucks she'd cost him, Plus this, and that, and more
Yet she attacks him every time, his hand comes near her
door

She's left some hefty scarring, when he braved, and came to near

In the hopes to win her kisses, because he loves her 'oh so dear'

Her would-be suitor eases close, he should run, he shouldn't linger

Unrequited his love shall stay, As the Lorikeet tears his finger

He pulls away to nurse his pain, for her beak is sharp and vicious

She sweetly sings to entice him back, because his blood, she finds delicious

She's had him now, oh numerous times, this man just never gave up

She thought he'd bought her a present, when he came home, with a pup.

How delicious she thought, another to tease, sadly she was mistaken

He transferred his love to the ball of fluff, her place in his heart, now taken

Her feathers drooped, she missed her toy, loneliness uninvited

He moved on, found happiness, where his love was now requited.

Celebrations

Deryn Pittar

CELEBRATIONS – a sestina

December passes, slow as snails, as the excitement builds.

No splendid tree, roof-topping tall, just a sawn-off branch

to prop and primp with tinsel strands and fairy lights,

a reindeer sleigh, a Christmas star, a jolly santa mask.

A gasp of fright, holding tight the ladder when it creaks.

Red pohutakawa blossoms - New Zealand's Christmas flower.

On Valentine's Day, red rose in hand I take my love a flower.

A stolen kiss in a secret place where our passion builds.'

Strands of weeping willows drape, dipping in the creek.

We climb from sight of prying eyes and straddle a branch,

Flesh presses flesh, then hand to mouth, her giggles she masks.

We fumble and kiss in the fading daylight.

The end of October, crisp nights and moonlight,

Spring in New Zealand, apples budding, pears in flower.

Trick-and-treat children, door-knocking in ghoulish masks

squeal in mock terror as their excitement builds.
In the park, false spider webs hang from a branch
and a 'spook street' sign is placed on the walkway by
the creek.

Midwinter, ice-cold, we wait by the creek
for Matariki to breach the horizon with her starlight.
We glimpse the rising constellation between branches.
In the hearth, driftwood burns and flames flower.
Within these warm walls the celebration builds.
Our Maori New Year that Covid can't mask.

On Yon Kippur our sadness wears a cheerful mask
Wherever you are, in concrete canyons or beside a
creek,
from today's sunset to tomorrow's nightfall, atonement
builds.
We wear white for the angels and praise the light.
Beg God for favours and let forgiveness flower
We pause and remember our sins today, offering an
olive branch.

Gifts exchanged, goodwill is spread, to every family
branch
With songs of praise and swaying delight our sadness is
masked
We hope and pray that over man's evil goodness will
flower.
The dancers move down the path to cross the creek

We join the parade, celebrating Diwali, the festival of light.
Health and wealth our annual plea and so our prosperity builds

Families gather, every branch, young ones dash, old bones creak.
The celebrations mask ancient feuds now blessed by bright sunlight.
Gifts are exchanged, friendship flowers and so our community builds.

Devastation

Johanna M Rae

I told you to go
But, my heart whispered stop
Please stay
Don't ever leave

I watched you drive away
Toward dreams and opportunity
Happiness so deserved
Everything you needed

I was glad for you
But, I was devastated for me
My soul aches
Empty and lost

Creativity

Sally Pugh

There is an undeniable truth
That is all too often
Misunderstood.
It is cloaked in the phrases "I'm not creative",
"I don't have a creative bone in my body",
But I see this truth
Every day
In the construction corner
In the sandpit
Anywhere children are playing.
All children are creative.
Every child has an innate desire
To create.
Whether it is making up stories,
Building cities and bridges
Going to the moon
Painting rainbows and families
Or making mud pies.
We are all born creative.
Every single one of us.
Creativity is not subject to talent.
Creativity is not restricted to a few select people.
Creativity is not limited or restricted to
Age,
Gender,

Race,
Or anything else that stops you from doing something.
Creativity is as much a part of you as you yourself are.
You were born a creative being.
You can't lose it.
It's still inside you.
Waiting for you to say,
"Hey, let's play".

A Winters Blue Moon

Deborah Carter

Lazily swinging to and fro
My garden swing-seat swings
Above us, a sky of diamond stars
Moths fluttering powdered wings.
Heat 'n' humidity powers on
From the New Year's sun filled day
The January moon climbs slowly
To chase the sun away.
The Moon doth turn around the Earth
And the Earth around the Star
From North and South to East and West
We see it from afar.
Passing stars, galactic clouds
On land it pulls the tide
To Northern hemisphere's winter sky
Where you're huddle warm inside.
For icy cold's the weather there
So very few will spy
The beauty of the Luna light
As the blue moon fills the sky.

Even Darkness Must Abide

S.N. Goldensnoot

It's always ending
Always dying
We're pretending
Ever trying

Buried still in spite of this
Which facts and scientists can miss
Belief that reason cannot chide
A faith that doubt itself abides

When such faith goes as ribs do show
The creature eats itself to live
And makes another step
Knowing there is nothing left to give

With stomach empty, nearly dead
There's hope of fullness yet ahead
It leads the beast to the next feast there
And even hunger must adhere

Come the mercy of winter's sun
The peace sustained for trees as seeds
When war is lost and talk is won
And white flags fly for the enemy's needs

The dog who licks the hand that smacks
The nearly-lethal heart attacks
The love that mothers demonstrate
Hate itself must tolerate

It's nearly ending
I'm nearly dying
I quit pretending
But not trying

For there is a flame
Substance in abyss
If only that
I'm sure of this

That in the face of fading stars
And turmoil in this termite jar

There's a kind of light that lives inside

That even darkness must abide.

I Don't Want to Miss a Thing

Clare Erasmus

I don't want to miss a thing
From the time you were a
sparkle in my eye,
The butterfly kisses
and the soft warm embrace.
Your smile is the engine of my heart
Eagerly driving me
Yet racing through time.
Oh, I don't want to miss a thing.

Looking on as you carve your way,
The corners you turn and
The reversing as you anguish
And I hold your hand
from near and far.
Your eyes are mirrored in me,
My reflection in you,
I hold you in my heart in each step
Oh, I don't want to miss a thing.

The compass is there
To guide you and lead you.
Your moral domain is your core
With your head and your heart
It's you that brings me life
Not I that brought you into
The world with all its
Tribulations and triumphs
Oh, I don't want to
Miss a
thing.

What the Stars Know

Chanelle Muirhead

There was so much left to tell you.
Instead, I whisper it to the night sky,
hoping you can hear me
among the stars.

Fully Pimped

Andrene Low

Another full circuit completed. Rims spinning,
double exhaust hammering at chests.
Stubbie-jumping subwoofer filling eardrums.

Momo in hand and underfoot, she's who he is.
Her gleaming body reflects his pre-fab image.
Dark and sinister at just seventeen.

Every bolt's a piece of him, the vanity
plate a fusion of overtime and stolen beer,
of going without and slogging.

Texts tell of start times and empty streets.
One step ahead, one street away, one hour too late.
The thrill of the race, the kick of getting away.

A slag in sprayed-on pants marks the line.
His eyes lock onto her t-shirt, held high
above her head. Ready to drop.

He misses its fall. Blinded by blue and red.
His rear-view mirror chocker full of a
porcine show of strength.

He floors it; chasing, drawing level, pulling away.
Away from the competition, away from the pigs.
Towards freedom and suburbia.

First corner, attacked in a kerb-skimming slide,
just maintained. Line-up achieved, then lost.
Parked car, fish tail, screeching tree.

The bark rushes him, crowding his vision before
he flies like an angel through the windscreen
to lie like a doll on the road.

Unrequited

Stacey Broadbent

Your eyes they are so blue
So deep I could just drown.
Your hair dark like the night sky,
Though others might say brown.

Your smile could light up any room,
Filled with so much charm.
Oh how I wish it was I
Who could be on your arm.

You make me laugh, you make me smile,
You bring a tear to my eye.
For to you I am but no one,
Just a person passing by.

You know not that I'm here
Awaiting your attention.
For even but a moment
Of your love and your affection.

So I shall sit and wait,
Admiring from afar.
Until the day you notice
I'm forever where you are.

Low Tide on Omaha Beach

Susan Howard

Footsteps in the sand are squeaking in tune
    with the incoming sea wash.

Distant laughter and our heavy breathing
    eventually join hands.

Shells crunching underfoot, signpost
    the familiar walk.

Though the scallop
    waiting for the high tide,
        is contemplating a happier future.

Listen

Johanna M Rae

Close your eyes and listen
Do you hear what I hear
Could that be the arctic beast
Tiptoeing past your ear
Melodious caterwaul
The song of the wind
Dancing on silver foot
My dreams to rescind

Battering my ego
Crash, whoosh, it arrives
Listen to the sound
Of my heart as it cries
A swirl of cold dread
Listen if you dare
Wailing and whistling
A scornful taunt upon the air

No mercy for the wicked
No honour for the brave
Don't let it take my dignity
In some convoluted rage
Listen for it has quieted
Not a whisper, nor a hiss
Where are you wind, don't toy with me
Leaving the promise of your kiss

Stripped bare and now impatient
I gather all my wit
How dare that gusty thief
Escape without remit
Incredulity grows rampant
I listen but there is naught
No scathing howl to remind me
Of this battle I have fought

I stand here rife with expectation
Is that all wind, are you done
Listen to the sound of my victory
Surrender, I have won

99% Nothing

Warren Greive

Three in one danced
Cosmic powers that
Spun eternal belonging
And from that community
From that communication
From that fellowship
From that love
the word spoke,
From nothing
Atoms of 99% space
arranged themselves
Galaxies composed themselves
Earth formed
And the godhead
saw it was good,
The word spoke
in power again
and then from matter
Atoms, nuclei and electrons
was formed a living
99% nothing:
65% water
65% oxygen
18% carbon

16% protein
16% fat
100% loved
100% belonging
welcomed home
to Father, Son and Spirit.

Mirror Boy

Will Alexander

There was once a boy
who climbed through the mirror
Where to his astonishment he found
Everything was exactly the same
Except for the other way round

Rainbows come from a Threatening Sky

Hope Mendelssohn

Rainbows come from a threatening sky
Colourful thoughts from the fear inside
The golden cage that you press against
Hoping for the freedom of the birds outside
Find your freedom from the spirit inside you
Find your key to unlock that door
Let not the darkness that surrounds you
Engulf you as a threatening wave on an ocean
shore
Find the shells that sing to your heart
The rainbow shells with their messages of love
Listen to the gulls circling all around
With their words of wisdom, melodies abound
In heaven not in a man-made cage
Listen to the sage who'll tell you
Rainbows come from a threatening sky.

A Fresh Start

Stacey Broadbent

An ember
A glowing light
A spark of what's to come.
One step
Is all it takes
To unravel what is done.

An idea
A fleeting thought
But one you can't let go.
One choice
Is all it takes
To reap what you sow.

An image
Is ringing clear
A future fair and bright.
One leap
Is all it takes
To bring your dreams to light.

Cherished

Clare Erasmus

Sprinkles of sunshine
Pirouette all around.
Whimsical thoughts,
Bundles of blossoms
And airbrushed dreams
Cherished.

Flutters of hope,
Buckets of peonies,
Looking toward
Sunsets on hills.

Gentle embraces,
Moments held tight,
In laughter and whispers
That dance through the night.
Soft as the moonlight,
Bold as the dawn,
Treasures and memories
To keep growing on—
Cherished.

Afterword

As we close this anthology, we are reminded of the beauty and power of words to weave connections between hearts and minds. Each contribution has been a thread, intricately woven into a tapestry of thoughts, emotions, and ideas, creating something truly unique and meaningful.

To our New Zealand authors, thank you for sharing your voices, perspectives, and creativity. Your words reflect the essence of Aotearoa—its landscapes, its people and its stories—and have drawn us together as a community of writers. This anthology celebrates the shared spirit and talent that flourishes across our country.

May these poems continue to inspire, spark conversation, and remind us of the enduring bonds that poetry creates, not only in words but in connection.

Arohanui, and thank you for being part of this journey.

Clare Erasmus and Stacey Broadbent